Titles by *Langaa*

An Evil Meal

of Evil

Kehbuma Langmia

Langaa Research & Publishing CIG
Mankon, Bamenda

Publisher:
Langaa RPCIG
(*Langaa* Research & Publishing Common Initiative Group)
P.O. Box 902 Mankon
Bamenda
North West Region
Cameroon
Langaagrp@gmail.com
www.langaapublisher.com

Distributed outside N. America by African Books Collective
orders@africanbookscollective.com
www.africanbookscollective.com

Distributed in N. America by Michigan State University
Press
msupress@msu.edu
www.msupress.msu.edu

ISBN: 9956-558-90-7

This play was first performed in 1997 at the Ecole Normale
Superieur, Yaounde, Cameroon, by the ENS Bambili Bilingual
Letters students on internship in Yaounde. Since then the play has
had several other performances in the North West Province of
Cameroon.

DISCLAIMER

Contents

Act I

Act II

Dedication

In memory of my beloved grandfather

Pa Joseph Foncham.

Foreword

I am greatly honored that Kehbuma Langmia has asked me to write a foreword to his play, *An Evil Meal of Evil.* However, I understand the choice, as the play was hatched right under my watch; I watched it go on stage for the first time; and I read and edited the final draft. I cannot go into the long close relationship between Kehbuma and me that relates to the conceptualization of this play. Nonetheless, in one of our many corridor conversations when we lived in the same dormitory at École Normale Supérieure (ENS), in Yaounde, Cameroon, in 1994, we shared our individual experiences with witchcraft growing up as boys in the village. The one thing that marked our experiences was how much we knew about the 'dirty cult' of witchcraft from the constant education by our parents and the various strategies, which each of our fathers gave us to enable us survive the wrath of blood-drinking witches and see the light of adult youth. While we were both waiting for graduation from ENS, Langmia came up with the idea of a play on witchcraft for three reasons: 1) we were constantly apprehensive, as we would attract jealousy upon graduation and join the highest echelon of civil servants in Cameroon at the young age of 29; 2) we had lost some classmates in quite mysterious circumstances while we were in ENS and that heightened our awareness about the looming witchcraft; 3) we had a lot of time in our hands and the actors that Langmia found, students of the Bilingual Letters Major in ENS Bambili were having a year-long immersion French course in Yaounde and agreed to perform the play. Langmia and I coordinated the rehearsals and the play was performed eventually in the main auditorium of the ENS Yaounde in 1996.

After Kehbuma Langmia revealed the mysterious powers of the menopausal women of the Takumbeng in his first play, *Titabet and the Takumbeng,* he has taken one courageous step forward to confront yet another fetishist mystical powerhouse, the most dreaded incredible practice in African mythology – the multifarious existence and evolution of cannibal witchcraft, locally called 'munyongo' in Cameroon indigenous languages and socio-cultural discourse.

While *Titabet and the Takumbeng* "imaginatively chronicles a true historical event" (Plastow vi), *An Evil Meal of Evil* is a bold indictment of a chronic perpetration of institutionalized psychological torture by witch squads who have preyed on the goodwill livelihood of people in every nook and cranny in Cameroon and in many other places in Africa. It is a vivid portrayal of the victimhood of those who believe in traditional African rites and customs, which have been taken hostage by a few greedy cannibals who hunt blood and organs of innocent people to use for the mystical rituals of their underworld practices.

On a daily basis, Africans, men, women and young adults like Dohbani in the play find themselves confronted with questions of the mysterious disappearance, death, illness or handicap of a loved one, a friend, a neighbor, a common man on the street, a rich and wealthy person or even a major community leader. *An Evil Meal of Evil* is a depiction of family drama involving the chauvinistic greed of Njekebim and the cannibalistic ambitions of his wife, Nahwubly, a loyal member of the occultist underworld, Nda'saah. The lesson espoused here is that nobody is completely trustworthy in the community. In everyone's lifetime, there are separate but similar stories to tell about witches within one's family – mother, aunt, father, uncle, sister or brother – and indiscriminate witchcraft and witch doctors around the village that, in one way or the other are deemed to have involved themselves in mysterious circumstances that led to human tragedies such as death, long-term illness or handicap. Therefore, Langmia's confrontation of this predicament through theatre is the credit, which this play earns.

In 1978 at the age of eight, I watched a worrying look on my father's face, as he explained to his male children in a family gathering that "You should run and hide in the bush every time you meet any of the members of the 'Kwih-fon' because he will eat your heart and drink your blood if you let him meet you face-to-face." When I became ten years old, my father made it an evening fireplace tradition to warn my siblings and me about "witchcraft looming over young children and the youth in the village and the danger of dying young and working as laborers in the underworld plantations of 'munyongo' people." His warnings only reinforced the little gossip I had many times with my child friends on the soccer playground in school and at home about the existence of "witches" from the supernatural world who kill and eat people mysteriously. At fifteen, my father enlisted the services of a strong and powerful 'medicine man' from Foumban in the French-speaking West Province. He was called Massa Nganjeu, a 'native doctor' who was renowned for 'protecting' people with talismans and chasing and casting witches, devils, ghosts and reincarnated beings' from many villages. He planted a 'medicine pot' in the entrance to my father's compound, made three-to-four little razor blade cuts on the joints on everyone's body, then he made the boys carry little tea sachet-size bags of talisman to protect them from being killed awake or asleep for life. We were not to take a shower for the following three days or damage the strength and effectiveness of the talisman. Generally, this is the cultural aura that characterizes life and the cosmos of my village and many others in Bamenda in the northwestern region of Cameroon. So, is there any place in Africa where one wouldn't hear of witchcraft or witches killing people and 'eating' their organs or 'drinking' blood or making them disappear mysteriously and do forced labor in underworld plantations of witches?

The subject of the play is rooted in a tradition of taboo regarding human misfortune and death in the African traditional cosmos. Death and bad luck used to be an acceptable subject of taboo in traditional African communities up to the end of the pre-colonial era when it was 'normal' for traditional governing bodies who represented the power structures to be called 'secret societies' that perform varying rituals within the communities, sometimes including human sacrifices, human blood, or human organs. Normally, people who became members of these 'secret societies' were not to live among ordinary people and be seen "with the naked eye" because of the secret pacts they have entered into in order to become ritualists for the welfare of the community. With the advent of western civilization and the influence of its power structures, the secret societies evolved into diabolical bodies representing differing ambitions and objectives of their members. In Langmia's play, Ngangkwetbun and his boss, Buhkap represent this breakout while Nahwubly is the greedy, treacherous and gullible villager who falls in the web of the occultists. This pattern explains why there is no accident in human tragedy in the world of *An Evil Meal of Evil*. From that point, death and human misfortune in traditional African society ceased to be natural and any such instance become associated with witchcraft and mysterious cannibalism known in Cameroon as "Munyongo" or "Nda'saah" in *An Evil Meal of Evil.*

Therefore, a Cameroonian audience in particular and an African readership in general will be quite familiar with the story line and the lessons, which the play attempts to teach. Dohbani's plight in the play would quickly remind many an African of the similar stories around his or her community – a mother or a father is accused of 'eating his or her own embryos or born children using witchcraft.' Also, Ngangkwetbun represents the king cannibal whose name alone sends a chill down the spine of any young man who would like to survive up to his twenties in most traditional African villages. Thus, the play raises a serious set of issues relating to greed, jealousy, power, poverty, sexism and male chauvinism. The play also raises the following questions: Who is to blame for witchcraft in Cameroonian communities? What can be done about it? Should it be allowed to feed on itself? If yes, what about the innocent people who get hurt before the evil ones meet their doom?

The play shows that Langmia has a great sense of language function, especially the expression of meaning in multilingual resources put at the disposal of the various characters. The central language of the play is English but it carries a local color or it portrays heavy appropriation of the English language. In this sense, meaning is not in English syntax as it is traditionally expressed in the English language; it is meaning as expressed in indigenous African languages such as Mungaka in the play. The reader finds the effectiveness of cynicism and mockery through extended rhetorical questions, open questions and statements put into question form. Thus, Dohbani's questions to his fiancé, such as 'So you rejected me because my trousers were all torn?' The non-African audience might mistake the dialogue in the play for incoherent thoughtless utterances or unnecessary dramatic discourse. But responding to a question with a question is a typical and an effective speech habit among African indigenous people that conveys the frustrations of the actors with the subject they are discussing. Apart from that, the use of Pidgin English does not suggest low educational status on the part of the characters who use it; but it reflects the function of the meaning intended – a linking language between people of different ethnic backgrounds in Cameroon.

I commend Kehbuma Langmia for finding a contemporary literary means such as theatre to confront, admonish and highlight the plague of the taboo of witchcraft, which has consumed his people for more than a century and which will only get worse in the future.

Isaiah Ayafor, PhD
Professor, English Composition and Professional Writing
Montgomery College, USA

Work Cited
Plastow, Jane. "Foreword," *Titabet and the Takumbeng* by Kehbuma Langmia. Bamenda: Langaa Research & Publishing, 2008. v-ix.

Act I

Dramatis Personae

Njukebim, Father of Sunyin

Nadoh, Mother of Sunyin

Sunyin, Marries Dohbani

Nahwubly, Mother of Dohbani/member of Nda Saah

Dohbani, Husband to Sunyin

Nukemih, Member of Nda Saah

Nganglooti, Member of Nda Saah

Ngangdong, Member of Nda Saah

Buhkap, Leader of Nda Saah

Ngangkwethun, Member of Nda Saah

Loohfah, Member of Nda Saah

Njenumeh, Seer of the village

Toohtu, Servant to the seer

Ngangtum, Town crier

Ma Petema, Sunyin's neighbor

Joshua, Reverend Pastor

Scene 1

Njukebim, Sunyin's father is in his "Talih."

(Dohbani arrives bearing a jug of palm wine to begin traditional wooing rites for Sunyin. Njukebim calls out for Sunyin to introduce her to Dohbani, her future husband. Sunyin bursts into tears in resentment.)

Njukebim
(Alone in his 'Talih')

Wonderful! The sun is almost coming out from its shell. I believe Dohbani could not have been deceiving me when he proposed that he would come this morning and take Sunyin who is now giving me a lot of trouble. She is already grown up with hair on her armpit. It's time for me to get rich! She must go! But, first, I must have my money. Ah! Money! The one thing that can make men happy, even the jailed. I want a big stomach like my friends. Who is Sunyin to decide for herself? I am her father *(hitting his chest)*; even her mother has no control over her. If Nadoh were to go away, she would not follow her. She would stay back here with me. Therefore, I have power over her... But where is this Dohbani? The young have no regard for the old nowadays!

(As he picks up his calabash, rope and cutlass in preparation to go to the farm, Dohbani arrives carrying a jug calabash of palm wine. Njukebim helps him put down the calabash then looks for his traditional cup and immediately gulps down two cups.)

I thought you might have been beaten by an antelope.

Dohbani

No! Not at all! I got up at very early in the morning, arrived at my first palm wine tree at cock crow only to find that rain had diluted the original content. So I dashed to Nkob-Ndeng at Njenmoh to collect this one especially for you. Your tongue has accepted the taste, I think.

Njukebim
(Drinks more)

This 'Mbuh', it has been a year since I tasted a drop. Here in 'Bu,' we tap only the raffia. Our tongues have rejected its taste. It now has a negative appeal and only strangers find it satisfactory. So

4

what news do you bring from Ntisong?

Dohbani

The spread of chicken pox has affected almost all the youth in our community. You can even see it on my body. (*Showing his back to Njukebim*) That is why I keep on scratching my body... Oh! I almost forgot. (*Laughing*) Something interesting happened. Sumson was disgracefully beaten by his wife the other day.

Njukebim

Sumson! That old drummer with whitlows on his fingers? What was the matter? (*Laughing mockingly*)

Dohbani

She complained that Sumson had consumed all her corn foo-foo in the past dry season. Now that the rain has come and men are supposed to cut the grass on their wives farms and cultivate together with them, Sumson spends all his precious time in the 'Buh' bar conversing with other women.

Njukebim

I, Njukebim, can never be beaten by a woman, a thing that sits down before she urinates? Eh! They are only good for caring for their husbands and bearing children. Whether they bring forth ten or more children, they have to care for them. Let me wait for about ten minutes without Nadoh bringing my usual morning foo-foo, then we will see whether she is the head of this household or me. Since when did wives begin to beat their husbands? The world must be turning upside down. This same Sumson could not even wrestle during the last fight with Wabila. Has he not got his gods at home?

Dohbani

(*Laughing*)

His gods are as weak as himself... Now, to the pertinent issue. Where is she?

Njukebim

I'll call for her. Let us resolve the issue before she comes.

Dohbani

(*Giving him money*)

I've borrowed this from my friend. It should not be surprising to you that I've brought only half the sum you requested to oil your lips. More will come during the traditional wedding ceremony.

Here it is. (*presenting it*)

Njukebim
(*Counts, shrugs his shoulders to show partial satisfaction*)
When she comes, speak like an elegant young man whose blood is strong and active.Sunyin! Sunyin!!

Sunyin
(*Answering from offstage*)

Bah, Bah!

Njukebim
(*Directing her to sit beside Dohbani*)
As from today, you are no longer a girl but a woman. Look here! This is now your husband. (*She bursts out weeping*) Stop crying. I say stop that (*getting up*). Go now and reflect on your new status because as from next month you'll have a new home. (*She gives a loud cry as she exits*).

Dohbani
Maybe she is unwilling.

Njukebim
Ah! You talk as if you are ignorant. She is pretending! She is deeply happy at heart because she will now begin to experience and enjoy the sweet things of the flesh. Her action is similar to the one displayed by her mother when I trekked to 'Beh' to take her hand in marriage. Her mother even gave a much louder cry than she has done.

Dohbani
I think she is afraid of me at the moment. Her shyness is still evident. Let me return to my home to start preparing for the big wedding night.
(*Exits*)

Njukebim
Women are unpredictable. She will now go and tell everything to her mother instead of keeping it to herself. But I am the head of the family and I'll do all in my powers to convince her mother; so that she can in turn convince all parties involved to accept the marriage proposal. (*Drinks another cup of palm wine*)
(*Enter Nadoh*)

Nadoh
(Exasperated)
I cannot allow my young daughter to go into marriage. She is the only child I now have to work with me in the farms. You sent her brothers and sisters to stay and work with your other brothers, sisters and mother. Now you want to send Sunyin away too? She is going nowhere.

Njukebim
My dear wife, you can fall down just because you are shouting too much in your tirade. Have you lost your senses? Why not approach me in the most cordial and loving manner. Or have you forgotten that I am your loving husband (*goes forward to embrace her*).

Nadoh
I'll not give in to your flattery this morning.

Njukebim
Both of you want to rebel against me? … You better allow her to also experience the enticing joy of matrimony. You cannot even realize that when she goes away we will be free to be by ourselves most of the time?

Nadoh
She can acquire a partner somewhere else; not Dohbani whose mother is unbearable. In Ntisong, people have gone as far as accusing her of practicing witchcraft. They call her the consumer of human flesh.

Njukebim
I don't expect you to open your soft ears to those hard and cunning words that only demonstrate jealousy among women. Men hardly find themselves in that mess. Early this morning, I went to Njenumeh who looked critically into the marriage of Dohbani and Sunyin. According to him, their marriage will be long lasting and prosperous. I spent a lot of money just to get things all right. Nadoh, you are my wife, aren't you? … It would be hypocritical for me to hide the truth from you. For close to twenty years that we've been together, what is usually the topic of our discussion before we retire to bed? Are my proclamations and predictions ever false? God almighty is directing me. He directs me where to put my next step, sit on somebody's stool, detect the cause of a

7

thunder and, more importantly, to foretell the future of my family. Who are you, therefore, to dispute with God almighty and Njenumeh, the Seer? If they have agreed on the marriage of Dohbani and Sunyin, wouldn't you be proud to be a grandmother and me a grandfather someday?

Nadoh

Of course, I'll even be more proud amongst my friends to have a child who addresses me as grandmother. Without further doubt, I am convinced that with God almighty and Njenumeh all will be well. Look at the case of 'Tanuketih' whom the Seer said thunder would one day strike. And it did. He stopped the rain from disrupting the death celebration of 'Ngangju'. That entire day the weather was extremely bright so much so that people drank, got drunk and forgot their calabashes while some women went back to their husband's homestead late in the night. (*both of them burst out laughing*)

Njukebim

Go now and think up the strategy you will employ to persuade Sunyin to agree to the marriage proposal. After all, you are a woman and you know all the tactics. Go and convince her to agree before I step in.

(*Exit Nadoh*)

Njukebim

(*Drinks another cup of palm wine*)

Ha! Ha! Ha! She thought she was very clever! Ha! Ha! Ha! I've proven to her that I am the head of this household. My decision is final. She knows nothing of the little sum of money I got from Dohbani and neither can she dispute the lie that I went to Njenumeh to consult on Sunyin and Dohbani's case. Her brain is too small. Only words have completely overcome the anger of Nadoh into accepting this marriage. We could have equally postponed the matter until one of her children returns to help her in the farms but now she will till the soil alone while I enjoy my money.

(*Exits*)

Scene 2

Sunyin has been married for over a year now.
*(She finds Ntisong very comfortable and is seen in this scene
looking after the husband by removing jiggers from his toe and
also picking lice from his head. The mother of Dohbani,
Nahwubly, interrupts by putting a marriage chain on her neck.)*

Dohbani
(Seated and stretching his leg on Sunyin's lap)
When shall we be free from such inconveniences, Sunyin? The
land we live on and till is rebelling against producing more food.
Yet jiggers want to feed on my dry body. Last year the yams and
cocoyams at Njenmoh wept bitterly for not being able to produce
their young ones simply because there was no moisture. The world
is turning upside down. My wife, where shall we go? Aie! Aie!
Aie! You did not sharpen that short stick well. *(Scratching the spot
where he has just felt pain)*. If you don't remove it painlessly, know
that you'll hardly sleep in the night because I'll keep on scratching
it on your body.

Sunyin
Then I will get up and sleep somewhere else.

Dohbani
Sleep somewhere else? Did I hear you well? Are you in your right
senses? Look, I am the one that has married you and not the other
way round. Paying bride price on your head was in order for me
to use you well until you are worn out.

Sunyin
Did I hear you well.

Dohbani
Bend down and remove my jiggers before I pounce on you. *(She
continues to remove the jiggers)* I am the sole owner of your body and
can even x-ray it like a midwife on a patient. *(Sunyin sobs and Dohbani
starts to console her)* ... Sunyin stop crying. Have you forgotten that
I am your darling husband? We've been married now for a while,
yet both of us seem to behave like two opposing walls that cannot
embrace or speak to each other. You have not inquired about my
father? Not even whether I have brothers and sisters and so on.

You've remained silent like a goat chewing its cud. Sunyin, tell me, who besides me has ever proposed marriage to you?

Sunyin

You remember that you were the very first boy to chase me especially when both of us met in the stream?

Dohbani

Ouh! Ouh! Ouh! So this is how you can retain past events in your little brain? Can you also recall how you used to behave like a queen? As if you would only get married to somebody from the city. Chei, chei! Why did you behave to me especially like that Sunyin?

Sunyin

You were as shy as flower buds in the garden. You hardly approached me! Instead you kept sending Nchoji, your mail van, whom I turned away like a woman rejecting a baby. In fact, I pitied your condition a lot. Your trousers were all torn revealing your dirty underpants.

Dohbani

You mean those were the negative impressions you had of me? Yes… No doubt… So you rejected me because my trousers were all torn? If I had better trousers I believe we could have had more than three children now.

Sunyin

Maybe.

Dohbani

Come now and embrace me so that all past demerits can vanish *(embraces her)*
    (Enter Nahwubly)

Nahwubly

You've started already? Are marriages nowadays made up of daily enjoyment in the form of sex and kisses? Dohbani, know that the essence of sex is solely to bring forth children. Don't indulge in it just for fun else, she may become exhausted and the fruits of her womb may deceive you one day with a cat. Two nights a month is enough. Now, daughter, come and show me your neck. *(Puts the brown chain of married women on her neck)* Henceforth, you are a woman to till and own a farm. Let it not escape your neck, else you shall never find a single moment of pleasure. Look well after your husband. He is the narrow-minded and childish type who is experiencing sex for the first time. And you, Dohbani, show your best character to this young woman whose virginity has never been violated. She is noted for her humility and quiet composure. Any questions before I go to my meeting?

Dohbani

Nothing, Mama.

(*Exit Nahwubly*)

Sunyin

Where is the usual meeting of Nah?

Dohbani

I don't know it myself but I presume it should be where they borrow money to pay for their farms during the cultivation season.

Sunyin

How long will she be there?

Dohbani

Very long. They exhaust many vast topics concerning farming before they return to their various households.

Sunyin

(*Changing the subject*)

My inner spirit informs me that I'll be the only guest in your chamber and no intruder shall be welcome.

Dohbani

You mean you'll be my only wife till death transports me to heaven. No way. Some of your counterparts could easily invite my loving eyes to meet them. One never knows; I intend to keep at least six of you.

Sunyin

If that should be your intention then today let darkness and daylight be my judge: Our marriage will be very uninteresting. I have extremely negative feelings about polygamy and cannot in any way encourage it since it breeds envy. Therefore, I remain the only recognized mistress of this house and the family at large.

Dohbani

Any woman who has a negative attitude towards polygamy is, strictly speaking, a selfish creature who shows false loyalty to her husband. If there is a divorce, the husband will be like the wounded lion in the forest searching for its claws. Experience has shown

11

and reason has proven, too, that many monogamists usually die early for various reasons. Then the so-called only wife pretentiously demonstrates agonized sympathy by putting on the black gown. When the mourning period is over, she reverts to the age of sixteen and starts to look for another catch. Monogamists are simply a group of poverty-stricken men who can only afford to marry one wife. I cannot be like that. I shall marry many of you.

Sunyin
(Weeping and lamenting)
I have married a husband who desires more sex and children than love. This means that he has no iota of love for me as a person. *(Cynically)* Thank you very much!
(Exits)

Dohbani
I am a very wealthy palm wine tapper; an owner of a large farm. I am also recognized in the village as very powerful when it comes to wrestling. Would it therefore not be disgraceful and unmanly to marry only one wife who, hitherto, cannot even give birth? Besides, she cannot work in those farms alone. You see how women are envious. She is only shedding crocodile's tears. My decision is final. I must be a polygamist and beget many children to show my strength and influence in this village. Look at 'Piousy' living with a single wife and one child for nearly 22 years of marriage. Was he not publicly abused yesterday at the meeting? No one respects you if you are only married to one wife. Sunyin must accept my decision else she will spend the night on the floor instead of enjoying my sweet parts.

(Exits)

Scene 3

The members of 'Nda Saah'

(come in the following manner: Leading them is Nahwubly closely followed by Nganglooti, Ngangdong, Nukemih, Loohfah whose one leg is swollen, and Ngangkwetbun. They come in facing backwards in their special red uniform, a symbol of blood. When they are seated quietly, their master, Buhkap appears from backstage. He is huge and wearing a big gown. A bowl of blood and other mysterious articles are placed before him.)

Buhkap

(Holds the bowl of blood in his hands and looks up at the sky)
Blood! Blood! Blood!

Members

We are the bloodthirsty villains of this village.

Buhkap

Tanu, Ngangbebyu, Tabeb. Here once more are the seven bloodthirsty villains of this village. Send us your blessings and show us the way to all the evils deeds. Our fortunes lie with human beings. Tanu, Ngangbebyu, Tabeb, today we are here to welcome the contributions of Nahwubly who for quite sometime has not fed our sacred grove, 'Nda Saah', with any human being. Send to her the wisdom and power to choose the right person to help the others in the plantation. We know you are starving; human beings nowadays are becoming difficult to kill because they possess personal gods and talismans. Give us more powers to overcome their small strategies so that one day 'Nda Saah' will be proud of more human beings. Blood! Blood! Blood!

Members

We are the bloodthirsty villains of the village.

(Buhkap drinks from the bowl and passes it over to the members)

Buhkap

Where is Nukemih?

Nukemih

Here my lord. *(Rising)*

Buhkap

Last 'Nda Saah' you killed your husband and a handsome amount was given to you as a reward, part of which was to be used for more evil deeds. Tell us how far you've gone with the latter.

Nukemih

Your lordship, dear members of 'Nda Saah', I received the reward with honor and cheerfulness. My immediate aim was to go to the market, look for the most expensive and quick acting poisons for my victims. Unfortunately, I saw those that could be used only in food and drinks which I considered less powerful. But newly arrived from the village of Njamke are some drugs which when swallowed by us women, a sex encounter with a male partner would be his safe ticket to meet our other victims. (*They clap*) This, dear members, was bought with a large amount of money. I apply this each time I polish myself to look attractive to men, especially at night. I still have another one. This is specially meant to be deposited at the grave yard to be taken by the spirit of dead evil men. After a week, they can then provide me with a new ring which I'll wear on my right hand. Any person who greets me on the way will be afflicted with severe sickness and thereafter would die and join our victims. (*More cheers*) Your lordship, dear members, Loohfah can bear me witness.

Loohfah

Your lordship, dear bloodthirsty villains, the deeds of Nukemih has made her very famous in the village. So I also want to copy her example by adopting a similar technique. My secret room in our usual night club has yielded wonderful dividends. Last night, under the pretext that someone was anxiously looking for him, I brought in a young handsome boy who was dancing in the hall. There in the room his senses were completely ram shackled. When he was almost about to fall into a coma, I left to get my tools to amputate the well round head for sales abroad. Unluckily, somebody suddenly dashed in and gave him room to flee. I am told he is being treated in the hospital but I am sure that sooner or later he will join the plantation workers. (*Cheers*)

Buhkap

Blood! Blood! Blood!

14

Members

We're the bloodthirsty villains; we live by the flesh of human beings.

Buhkap

Where is Nahwubly?

Nahwubly

Here your lordship.

Buhkap

You either feed 'Nda Saah' with your only beloved son you promised us or you yourself can equally go to join the plantation workers since your children have all been killed except him.

Nahwubly

Your lordship, dear friends of evil men. I was preserving my only beloved son, Dohbani, to work for me and look after me as old age is fast drawing nearer. And now he has gotten married, meaning that he will instead devote more time to his wife than me.

Members

You're right. Let's kill him.

Nahwubly

Now, he has only a few moments to live in this world. He has been my companion, no doubt. But as you rightly said, your lordship, our 'Nda Saah' is hungry and wants somebody urgently to consume. My son is now ready.

Members

(*Cheers*)

Long live Nahwubly. Long live 'Nda Saah.' Down with Dohbani.

Nahwubly

I also wish that both Dohbani and his wife Sunyin be taken so as to increase the labor force in the plantation, your lordship. I don't know whether the council agrees with my proposal. She is unable to give birth because I mysteriously transfer her unborn children to our 'Nda Saah'. I feel it is necessary for her and her husband to join us.

Ngangdong

Your lordship, dear fellow villains, Sunyin is from a different compound where the grand father had fortified her with talismans and 'Nchop.' She is as hard as a rock against any evil force. But with Dohbani, as her husband, it may be easy since Nahwubly has influence over him.

15

Ngangwetbun

Moreover, she has been brought up in utmost good care. If she had been the daughter of Nahwubly, our influence would have been easy. However, I have one suggestion now that we intend to kill her husband. She would become a helpless widow and considering her youthfulness she will not stay husbandless for long. A young girl like her who has not given birth to any children would pick up another husband very easily. Since I am unmarried, I wish, on behalf of the mother of Dohbani, to marry her afterwards so that the children she will bear shall be transferred to 'Nda Saah! I don't know what you all think?

Nahwubly

I have seen that men would rush after Sunyin when her husband dies. This may cause problems especially as Ngangkwetbun has started to sharpen his sexual organs between his legs in readiness for Sunyin. If that should be the case, then I am not prepared to kill Dohbani.

Nganglooti

Then who will you give to 'Nda Saah' since you willingly agreed and our ancestors have sharpened their teeth in wait for Dohbani. I believe, at your age, you've already enjoyed the wealth of the world enough. You can equally give yourself.

Nahwubly

I will not!

Buhkap

Blood!

Members

We're bloodthirsty villains.

Buhkap

Who is our today's food for the ancestors?

Members

Dohbani the son of Nahwubly!

(*Nahwubly collapses*)

Buhkap

(*Sprinkles blood on her*)

Tanu! Ngangbebyu, Tabeb here is Nahwubly who last 'Nda Saah' meeting vowed to give you her son, Dohbani. Her other children and husband are with you. She has only Dohbani to give now. We shall do nothing else but take Dohbani as she had earlier promised. Tanu! Ngangbebyu! Tabeb! After Dohbani, she would be left alone in the world, and then when you next demand other food from us, she would therefore give herself. Send her back to us now because this is not her turn.

(*Nahwubly rises with the aid of the members*). Blood! Blood!

Members
(*Hitting their left legs*)
We are the bloodthirsty villains.

Buhkap
Who is the next guest of 'Nda Saah'?

Members
No other person but Dohbani, the son of Nahwubly

Buhkap
Let us now device a means to kill Dohbani in the next fortnight. Whether the wife commits suicide or performs an extraordinary act of life because we've taken her husband is of no concern to us. We met today with the sole purpose of taking Dohbani and not both of them. Therefore, Dohbani is our victim. Nukemih?

Nukemih
Your lordship.

Buhkap
(*Gives her certain herbs to eat and other traditional drugs*)
All these will help you to masquerade tomorrow morning as a cobra. You will hide in the thick grass at 'Njenmoh' near the path leading to Dohbani's palm wine tree. Immediately you spot his empty leg approaching, don't hesitate to bite. Bite deeply so that blood should flow. When he falls, escape to your household; there, you'll transform yourself back to your human form. Followed?

Nukemih
Your lordship, I'll do it well.

Buhkap
At our next meeting, due in a week's time, when Dohbani is buried, a special commission will be set up to receive him from the grave. But for our usual annual meeting, Nganglooti, it will be your turn. You should henceforth start to contemplate what method you will employ to give us your wife.

17

Nganlooti

Agreed your lordship.

Buhkap

Blood! Blood! Blood!

Members

We're the blood thirsty villains.

(*Exit*)

Scene 4

Dohbani and Sunyin are on stage.

(Dohbani is preparing his usual morning attire for palm wine tapping. Sunyin is preparing corn foo-foo.)

Sunyin

My husband, after you have tapped your palm wine at 'Njenmoh' you will please join me at the cocoyam farm at 'Naku;' the grass is pretty tall and strong. I cannot weed alone.

Dohbani

Ah! *(gets up to go)* The sun is piercing my roof. I'm supposed to be close to 'Makup' by now. That would leave me only two kilometers to get to Njenmoh for my palm wine tapping. Reserve my own foo-foo in that big dish because I may return hungry. If I return when you've already gone to 'Naku', then I'll follow immediately. In the meantime let me hurry to 'Njenmoh.'

Sunyin

Husband, the foo-foo is ready. I don't see any reason why you wish to hurry. Your morning foo-foo is ready. Please my husband, stay and eat before you go. I can imagine you collapsing under the jug of palm wine because of hunger. And who will be blamed? Me as usual! Then, I'll have to desert my cocoyams and groundnuts in the farm to look after you in the hospital. Please, don't bring me ill-luck. Stay and eat.

Dohbani

Yes, you'll now pretend that you can care a lot for me. So I should abandon my palm wine in the farm for rain to spoil it only because of mere corn foo-foo, which I can equally eat after my job. Am I going to carry a hundred jugs of palm wine at 'Njenmoh'? Look, don't make as if you'll clean my anus before I go to the toilet. Don't bring me ill-luck. Reserve my foo-foo in that big bowl. When I return, I will devour it.

(Exits).

Sunyin

(Soliloquizing)

This action by my husband is making me confuse. Yesterday evening he could not sit for a long time with me near the fireside under the pretext that he was going to pass the night at a death celebration. I spent the night alone, rolling like a round pumpkin from one end of the bed to the other. Is this how he is going to behave towards me as a wife? Refusing to sleep with me and refusing to eat my food? Yes, he will say I have been unable to give birth, what is the use of sleeping with a woman whose womb is empty? Yei! But is he not foolish? My stomach protruded a bit and he was quite certain I was pregnant but after two months the baby disappeared. Whose fault was it? Maybe his sperms are too weak to form a baby in my womb. A weak husband pretending to be powerful! Yei! Now that he finds my meals tasteless, I am totally convinced that each time he goes to that his palm wine tree he stops at another woman's compound to eat his so called delicious food. Yei! Men are cowards and unpredictable. Since I am unable to convince him, I'll narrate all these events to his mother who will scold him on my behalf. I'll also leave a bigger portion of the farm for him to weed at 'Naku', so that he can demonstrate his manhood.

(Enter Ma Petema)

Ma Petema

Sunyin, I heard you talking to yourself. Is everything all right?

Sunyin

My sister, sometimes it is like that.

Ma Petema

What do you mean "sometimes it is like that?" Are you trying to tell me that you've become a mad woman in broad daylight?

Sunyin

No, Not really. I was just thinking and talking to myself about the way things are going on with our leaders in this village.

Ma Petema

Don't make me laugh, Sunyin. What things are going on in this village? You think I don't know why you were talking to yourself?

Sunyin

(Surprised)

What was I talking about? Tell me.

Ma Petema

Don't make as if you are instead angry at me now. Please direct your anger at him.

Sunyin

Who do you mean him? Please don't try to bring gossip into my house. I am just a young bride and I hear you go about nosing into people's business. Please stay away from us.

Ma Petema

Please, I am sorry if I've hurt you. It was not my intention. I simply wanted to know why someone like you will be angry with your beloved husband.

Sunyin

So you heard all what I was saying. Why were you pretending then? (Angrily) Leave my house now. I thought we were friends. But you seem to be untrustworthy.

Ma Petema

But I came to tell you….

Sunyin

I say leave me in peace *(sobbing)*.

(Exit *Ma Petema*)

(*Sound of a drum*)

What is the message of this drum! And why are my hands shaking, even my head, body and legs? But why should I bother? I come right from 'Bu' and can only share in the celebration of anything that occurs here. Could it be that the Fon is dead? Or are they calling on everyone to go and dig the road leading to 'Beh'? I cannot quite make this out. But let what be, be. Let me take my baskets and hoes to 'Naku' I can then sympathize or enjoy the news on my way.

Scene 5

Dohbani is brought in, dead.

(Sunyin is being restrained by Ma Petema as she sobs. The villagers follow after pastor Joshua.)

Sunyin
(Screaming and yelling)
Yelelelelelele! Yelelelelelele! Yelelelelelele!

Ma Petema
Hold yourself Sunyin.

Sunyin
(Breathing hard)
I hold my what? Where is my husband? Can you give my husband back to me?

Ma Petema
Hold it Sunyin, Hold it. Let's listen to the Pastor.

Sunyin
Who? Pastor? Is there a Pastor here? *(Moves to the Pastor)* Please tell your God to give back my husband?

Joshua
My dear sister, hold your peace. The Lord will listen to your pain. Just hold your peace for now.

Sunyin
What peace, Pastor? The peace to bury my young husband? The peace to live in hell as a widow without the one I love? Are you talking sense, Pastor?

Joshua
You shall meet with him again in the Lord's kingdom. Just hold your peace.

Sunyin
(Gives a loud cry, as she is restrained by Ma Petema)
Okay Pastor. If you think life is worth living tell your Lord in heaven to send him back to me. Please will you?

Pastor
I will sister. Can you just remain silent for us to pray so He can help you? *(Turning to the villagers)* Let's listen to the word of the Lord before we pray.

Blessed is he who is, who was and who is to come. The passage I have chosen for this sad meditation is from the gospel of Genesis chapter 3 verses 15-17. There, it is written:

"The Lord God then took the man and settled him in the garden of Eden, to cultivate and care for it. The Lord God then gave man this order: You are free to eat from any trees of the garden except the tree of knowledge of good and bad. From that tree you shall not eat; the moment you eat from it you surely doomed to die" This is the word of the lord.

Villagers

Thanks be to God.

Pastor

My brothers and sisters in the lord. Death has a place in our life. Many have puzzled, many have wept and have even kept all sorts of weapons to combat death. But death remains omnipotent. Everyone has to wait for his or her turn. Today is that of our brother Dohbani who was serviceable, loving, daring, generous and duty conscious. But the almighty and beloved father wants him at this hour. The beloved heavenly father has prepared a place for him in Heaven. Our lives are like the beautiful flowers in the garden with their beautiful colors. They shine in the morning but wither at night. We live like fruits on the tree. When the owner comes to harvest them, he chooses the ripe and sometimes the unripe. But one fruit does not jump and say take me or don't take me; it is the master who chooses those to take home. So, today the Lord has chosen our brother Dohbani. He could not go to tap his usual palm wine but to follow the Lord. We have no control over our lives but the almighty God. Therefore, let us not strain ourselves and swallow an elephant because God has taken our brother. We all will someday. We were doomed right from the incident in the garden of Eden. To you, Sunyin, *(moves over to her)* have peace of mind. Calm your internal spirit. Your husband is no more of this world. He is happy and jumping up and down with the angels in Heaven. In your widowhood don't think too much about your husband. Rather, pray for him to rest in peace. Amen

Villagers

Amen

Pastor

Let's now escort our brother Dohbani to his eternal home as we sing this dirge.

(Intones a local dirge as they move out with the body)

Act II

Dramatis Personae

Njukebim, Father of Sunyin

Nadoh, Mother of Sunyin

Sunyin, Marries Dohbani

Nahwubly, Mother of Dohbani/ member of Nda Saah

Dohbani, Husband to Sunyin

Nukemih, Member of Nda Saah

Nganglooti, Member of Nda Saah

Ngangdong, Member of Nda Saah

Buhkap, Leader of Nda Saah

Ngangkwethun, Member of Nda Saah

Loohfah, Member of Nda Saah

Njenumeh, Seer of the village

Toohtu, Servant to the seer

Ngangtum, Town crier

Ma Petema, Sunyin's neighbor

Joshua, Reverend Pastor

Scene 1

Following the death of Dohbani

(Members of 'Nda Saah' meet urgently to receive him. During the ceremony, signs and symbols are performed by Buhkap to mesmerize him and subdue him completely in their midst. They enter in their usual style.)

Buhkap

Blood! Blood! Blood!

Members

We're the bloodthirsty villains of the village.

Buhkap

Tanu, Tabeb, Ngangbebyu! We are assembled here this evening for what you already know. Your trap has caught the powerful animal. Nahwubly has fulfilled the mission, which was assigned to her. She has no other child now in the active world of living beings. When next your thirst has to be quenched or your throats have to be oiled, Nahwubly in her next turn will present herself to you. Congratulations to Nukemih who made it possible for Dohbani to be killed and buried. Let her now report to the assembly on how she achieved this.

Nukemih

Your lordship, dear members of 'Nda Saah'. My strategy as a woman of villainous intentions has enabled me to succeed. The pills given to me by your lordship were taken right here in our assembly. Early in the morning, in my sleeping room, I disguised as a large cobra, found a large hole in my house and headed directly for the path which leads to Dohbani's palm wine bush. There, I hid myself in thick grass and waited for about an hour when suddenly I heard footsteps approaching. I knew it was none other than him. Very precise were my teeth, as they found a safe way to penetrate through his leg. His hasty attempt to withdraw his leg only further deepened the wound. He fell down panting while I found my way home. I came back to my house and re-incarnated immediately to my human form. Your lordship, this is how I did it.

Members
(*Cheers*)
Buhkap

Let Loohfah, Ngangkwetbun and Ngangdong follow the path to the grave to bring Dohbani. (*Gives them certain magic webs and talisman which they will use in the grave*). At the grave, pray to our ancestors while hitting your left legs as usual and when you see him in front of you, call his name aloud seven times. Take him up, veil his head and bring him here. Go now as I order you. (*The three magic experts, tools in the hands of the ancestors, go to bring Dohbani from the grave. After a while they bring him veiled in a white cloth*).

Buhkap
(*Sprinkling blood on his head while raising his hands to the ancestors*)
Dohbani! Dohbani!

Dohbani

Eh! Eh!

Buhkap

You are heartily welcome to our meeting where we live on the blood of human beings. From now hence, you are to share in all our sacrifices of villainous intent. You will be instructed on what you are to do as a profession while you live on the farms. We do not have enough workers on our plantations. Our next human catch will be a student who should have completed secondary education. As for you Dohbani, you will be provided with digging tools to use in planting crops. You shall meet with other colleagues. This is the second world where all the evil men of this village and traitors dwell. Now we welcome you to 'Nda Saah' Dohbani! Dohbani!

Dohbani

Eh! Eh!

Buhkap

Here is your mother; she will give you your assignments as she holds your right hand.

Nahwubly

Dohbani, I am your beloved mother, Nahwubly, who is holding your right hand. I am responsible for bringing you to this happy world where we are looked upon as evil men and women. Back in the living world, you thought I was a truthful, loyal, honest, and

29

responsible mother. All those ideas you held about me were wrong. I declare to you now that I am a witch dealing with ancestors of the second world and you now form a part of that world. You thought your younger brothers and sisters died a natural death. They were all mysteriously killed by me. You will act like an elder brother to them on the plantation. Comfort them when they lament. Care for them. Guide them when they go astray. Be their watchdog. Share all your talents with them. I remind you again, I am your mother, Nahwubly, speaking. I wish you success and hard work. (*Sits down*)

Buhkap

Blood!

Members

We are the blood thirst villains. We wish Dohbani success.

Buhkap

Now Loohfah, Ngangkwetbun and Ngangdong, escort Dohbani to our secret room where he will rest. (*They take him out and return after*)

Ngangdong, it is your turn now to present Nahwubly with her valuable huge sums of money for giving us her son. (*Ngangdong gives her the money which she receives gladly*).

At our subsequent meeting due next year, Nganglooti, it will be your turn to give your wife. When you go home, think about the ways and means you will use to bring her to us. In the meantime, let us bring the meeting to a close as Nahwubly leads us out.

(*They leave the stage*).

Scene 2

Sunyin lies in her homestead, legs out-stretched.
(She reflects on what could have precipitated the death of her husband. The first sympathizer to share in her grief is Nahwubly. She has requested Njenumeh the seer to come and tell her the truth concerning the death of her husband.)

Sunyin
(Sorrowfully)

Here I am, a lonely girl experiencing widowhood. Here I am, looking pale as if I am a refugee abandoned in a foreign land. Here I am, with no child even to share in my sorrows or keep me company. This is the marriage which my parents wanted me to experience. Yes, this is the marriage. Having a husband only for a few unfruitful years? I see the world turning upside down. Everything is useless in my eyes. Here I am seated in a limbo as if God is dead to have chosen my destiny in such an agonized way. O! O! Where is my husband? Life has no more meaning for me. I am useless, lifeless and worthless. Sympathizers come and go, shedding tears that cannot restore my husband back to me. My mates who got married the same year like me now boast three to four children if not more. Where are mine? Has God also destroyed my womb? Yes, death has pronounced its verdict, allowing all the old men and women in the village only to send its whimsical hands to snatch away my youthful and beloved husband who had several plans in life. O! O! Death, why have you punished me like this *(weeps)*. When will I meet my husband again? Why can you not take me along to meet Dohbani, my beloved husband? But you wish to pour all the burden of suffering upon my head on this earth. My cocoyams at 'Naku', I have to work alone; my beans and corn in the farm, I have to cultivate alone and to consume all the produce alone!! O! O! Death you have betrayed me. *(weeps)* On the road as I go by people point fingers at me, some even murmur, "I pity that young lady" while they move happily with their children and husbands. Here I am, sitting in a limbo like a neglected child that cannot find a helper. My husband, please return to me. I mean now! Now! Now! *(Weeping)*
(Enter Nahwubly)

31

Nahwubly
(*Consoling her*)
My daughter, stop weeping. All will be well. Please, I beg you, stop weeping. Since your husband died, I have been very busy. I have consulted all the witchdoctors for answers to no avail. Please stop weeping. If you keep on weeping what am I going to do? Why do I have the ill-luck to bury my children instead of them burying me. Please let us not keep weeping. Let us pray for God's mercy, my daughter. (*weeps cynically*) Now tell me.

Sunyin

Tell you what?

Nahwubly

Is it true that someone told you that the only way to win my son's love was to charm him by putting something in his food?

Sunyin
(*shocked*)

Nahwubly

Please don't think I am the one asking. It is all out there.

Sunyin

Outside where? Who told you this shocking story?

Nahwubly

Well, I am only echoing what is out there.

Sunyin

Nahwubly, you think in your right mind that I, your daughter-in-law can do this?

Nahwubly

Don't ask me. I don't know. I thought you may have some clues.

Sunyin

What clues? I want to know the people who have been talking to you about this.

Nahwubly

I don't think it will be good for you to know.

Sunyin

Why not? I will like to know. Even if it is my best friend, I will still like to know. Except you have something to hide yourself, I see no reason why you will want to keep it secret.

32

Nahwubly
(Getting up to leave)
As I said it will not be good for you to know. Just think about it
and see what you can do about it.
(Exit)

Sunyin
This is now my fate. I will have to explain to everyone where
Dohbani has gone to. As a young widow no one will believe me.
I can't tell who is a friend or an enemy ever since my husband
died. Everybody thinks I have something to hide about his death.
Well, only time will tell. But where is old Njenumeh? Last night, I
requested that he come and reveal the cause of my husband's
death? Could he have forgotten or is he attending to other people?
Ah! These seers, they never keep to time. I am not convinced that
a cobra would sting somebody and in no time he would be dead.
I have never seen or heard of such a strange way of dying. Let
him come and reveal it to me. My parents trust him completely
and so do I. But where is he?
(Enter the seer with his servant)

Sunyin
Njenumeh, weti make-am you stay for come quick quick?

Njenumeh
… Mami? Plenti work be dei for me. Ehm… I di see wonder.
Na for yah you di stay?

Sunyin
Yes, papa.

Njenumeh
I nearly fall die for outside dei because trong spirit dem want
troway me for down. Yei, yei. Na di compound for your husband
dis again, I di ask am?

Sunyin
I say na yi this papa.

Njenumeh
You get lucky, Mami, I tell you. You for dong die long time as
dem bring you for yah. *(Sunyin gives him a chair)*
Me, I no di shidong for chair, Mami; I get my own chair. Toohtu!
Toohtu! *(The servant takes out an old torn mat from a bag and gives it to him)*
Give me! Hold this walking stick *(gives him his walking stick as he*

33

opens his bag and an absurd sound is heard) Heh! Heh! Mami, i go bad today. I tell you, come shidong near me, Mami. (*she draws her mat nearer*). Show me your hand. (*she shows her left hand*)

Sunyin

Papa, I dong forget for find out weti I go givam before you start.

Njenumeh

Mami, I no go take anything from you. Thing dem plenti weh I go tell you here today. If I take this money, some of dem go run. Na your hand this? Yeh! Yeh! (*takes out some cowries from the bag and throws them down on the ground*).

Mami, your husband no die go for heaven, you hear? Yi dey da so for this world.

Sunyin

For wusai? I fit go take yi papa?

Njenumeh

You no fit see yi with your eye. Mami, this world dong change plenti. Your case plenti plenti as I di see am for here. (*The servant approaches behind him*). You know something, Mami?

Sunyin

No papa!

Njenumeh

Dem kill your husband na for killam. (*Sunyin gives a cry but Njenumeh tells her to be cautious*). If you cry again I go go me back because some people weh dem kill your husband, dei da for dis compound. Some woman di stay near for this your house?

Sunyin

Yes, na mami for my husband dei for that house so (*pointing*)

Njenumeh

Na yi dong kill your husband. (*Sunyin exclaims*) No talk trong trong because you fit make-am I go me. Na yi bin go for that their meeting weh dem di collam say 'Nda Saah' and na yi take your husband make yi come di work for dei so that yi go get money. (*She screams*) Cover you mob. Da snake weh yi kill your husband, na woman for that meeting weh yi change for snake come bite you husband. Da Mami for your husband dong give all yi pikin dem all, and yi husband for da 'Nda Saah'. Now your husband di work all day and night for inside their farm. Dem dong givam plenti money for this big-big job weh yi doam. This money na

34

for kill more people dem. No talk all these things for some man, only for your papa and mama. Take this medicine chopam so that make dem no come beat you or take you when you comot for outside. (*Gives her some herbs to chew*). I say yi dong bad, Mami. Me, I di go na for go so. Ma melecine fit finish for yah, then dem come kill me since I dong tok all this thing for you. (*Parks his things and exits with his servant*)

Sunyin: I said it! I said it! Did I not say it? I am living amongst wild wolves and beasts. I did not know. My mother told me about the evil deeds of Nahwubly. I thought she was just being envious. Now I see! Now I see the true story of a wicked, inhuman and bloodthirsty woman. Chei! Chei! That somebody you share all joys and sorrows with should be so bright without and so dark within! Yes, this is the world in which we live. This world is full of human beings like Nahwubly. This world is full of betrayers, traitors and cunning fools like Nahwubly. And ignorant creatures like us are born into it! Oh God! How can you allow such people to live with us? I used to hear about devils, witches, dealers in the abstract world. I have seen it with my own eyes. My mouth used to be heavy whenever I would want to ask Nahwubly what had caused all her children to die so suddenly? Now I know. This was the cause. My husband was as naïve as I am; staying with a woman you call 'mother' whose sole aim is to suck human blood! I cannot stay in such a village. I will pack my things this night and leave without Nahwubly's knowledge and go to my parents in 'Bu'.

(*Exits*)

Scene 3

Njukebim and Nadoh are at home
(arguing about the fate of their daughter. Sunyin suddenly appears with all her belongings.)

Njukebim

My wife, what a sad omen for our daughter.

Nadoh

Don't mutter anything as sad because you are responsible for this everlasting ill-luck that has befallen my daughter. She is now forced in her youth to experience the life of a widow. Instead of experiencing the enticing pleasures of matrimony, she is going to gnash her teeth. Had I known! Had I known! I earlier disagreed with you about this marriage on the grounds that the family into which my daughter was marrying was full of people who practice witchcraft yet... *(weeps)*

Njukebim

Stop that. I warned you about making these kinds of assertions about people, which, frankly speaking, are miss-leading and completely false. Yes, when natural death occurs to somebody, you women quickly draw conclusions on the cause of the death.

Nadoh

Yes, now you reprimand me and forget your own assertions. Didn't you tell me that you had consulted Njenumeh and he foresaw the marriage of my daughter and Dohbani as prosperous, long-lasting, peaceful and hopeful? What has happened? What happened my husband? You want me to start distrusting the words of our most truthful seer in whom all confidence is entrusted?

Njukebim

You see how short-sighted and unreasonable some of you women can be? So you think Njenumeh is the almighty God who created mankind and can know when he or she has to die? Yes, you are really ignorant about many things. I cannot quite make it out why when death occurs such as in the case of Dohbani, you go around with less proven conceptions on supernatural causes. Look here my wife, in such cases, pray for the departed soul as we ought to do for Dohbani who is now seated at the right hand of God the father almighty. That is what we are told in church by pastor Joshua. We'll only meet with him on the judgment day. So, let us put away gossip and hypocrisy and pray for our daughter to withstand the challenges of widowhood.

Nadoh

You want my daughter to stay a widow? That is unheard of. She is too young. Moreover, she hasn't had any children yet. We should be looking for a second husband for her. I have been thinking of Tadoh who lives at 'Ngumbu'. He is a good wrestler, a good tapper and a good trapper of antelopes and other animals. Since the death of Dohbani, he has been very helpful to me. He has even offered to cultivate my farm come next farming season. Indeed, I find him fit enough to bring peace to the heart of my daughter. If you are in agreement on my choice, then all we need do now is to let Sunyin know of this proposal.

Njukebim

Certainly not. You don't seem to realize that Tadoh and I have not spoken to each other for two years. Have you forgotten my struggle with him over the farm at 'Njamke', and how the large farm has been abandoned for years because of no judgment? In the mean time he has been struggling to bring me down with his talismans and gods. I suggest 'Ngangbaki' who is my personal friend and who can settle bride price with ease.

Nadoh

You seem only to propose your personal friends who you believe can settle the bride price quickly. Do we need a duty conscious husband for Sunyin to take good care of her or do we need an individual who uses money as a wedge to maltreat his wife? I see. I now know the workings of your inner mind. You need only wealthy men who can fill your stomach with money. That basically is also the reason you gave my daughter to a hard-hearted devilish family that has now painfully reduced her, in her 20s, to a widow. What a world? (*weeps*)

Njukebim

Wipe those tears, woman. Are you accusing me of betrayal? If that is the case why not attack me directly? Why are you weeping? I know you are deeply contented because you can now influence your daughter to return and stay with you as you earlier affirmed.

Look, don't utter profanities in this house. Sunyin is not only your daughter but mine too. Both of us ought to be sympathetic to her situation but you believe this means crying out loud. Let us like responsible parents sit down and discuss the future of Sunyin. These accusations will neither help us nor her in the long run. If you continue to think that I am the cause of her downfall so be it. I believe what I did was done in good faith. But if you keep accusing me then you and your daughter can go elsewhere to look for peace. I can still get married to...

Nadoh

I bet you if I leave this house you'll not have any woman to replace me. Let me inform you. You think like the proverbial male that it is perfectly easy to get another woman when your wife is gone. Don't you know that when any wife leaves her husband's house people ask why she left? If I leave, no woman will come and do the things I do for you. Let me assure you that they would stare at you as a helpless bachelor. You seem to have forgotten the good things I have offered you in the past. Why did your first wife leave? Did I not lodge her sons and daughters before they became responsible citizens in this village? How many times did you use your hands on me, yet I forgave you and we moved on? My perseverance has been scornfully criticized by my mates. Yet, I have remained to serve you as a good housewife.

Njukebim

My wife, I hear you. Let us not quarrel. Let us be considerate and reasonable. Take my views as having been uttered thoughtlessly. Right now let us look at the pertinent issue of our daughter. I don't know whether she will still like Ngangbati. He was really a serious suitor too. But this should be looked into after she completes the mourning period for her departed husband. In the meantime we can both retire to bed. It is getting late. (*they rise to go when Sunyin makes her entry*)

Njukebim and Nadoh

What is wrong? (*helping her with her belongings*)

Sunyin

I am back! I am back home! I shall not continue to stay in Ntisong. Chei, chei! I have been chased out of the compound of Dohbani.

Njukebim and Nadoh
(In unison)

By whom?

Sunyin

It is a long story. But if you want to hear from me, know that Nahwubly is a witch!

Nadoh

Yah! What did I say? You call her a witch?

Sunyin

Permit me to reveal to you what has happened. I invited Njenumeh to look into the cause of my husband's death. I was having lots of sleepless nights and nightmares. For the first time he refused to receive a token of appreciation for his consultations. Njenumeh said that the death of my husband is unnatural, that villains have killed my husband. I wanted to weep but he stopped me and said the villains were around.

Nadoh

Chei! Chei! What did I say! Oh! Heaven help me!

Sunyin

That was not the end. He continued by saying Nahwubly is a member of the secret society 'Nda Saah'

Nadoh/Njukebim
(In unison)

'Nda Saah?'

Sunyin

My late husband told me of her meetings that usually take most of her time. When I inquired about the aim of these meetings Dohbani said she and other members discuss farming issues there. I became skeptical when I saw her going too often. Njenumeh said she gave Dohbani to 'Nda Saah'. Dohbani is working hard in their plantations, day in and day out.

Nadoh

Almighty father, send your holy spirit to change the mind of my husband. Let him not be the doubting 'Thomas'. When I told you about the character of Nahwubly, that she was a witch, you thought I was unreasonable. Believe the truth from Njenumeh, the great seer of the village.

Sunyin

Njenumeh had not finished as I expected but revealed again that all five of Nahwubly's children are working on the plantations of 'Nda Saah'. She was left only with her beloved son Dohbani. Since it was absolutely necessary that she give another relative to 'Nda Saah' or herself, she chose Dohbani. He went further to say the cobra that bit my husband on the path to his palm wine farm was a woman, a member of that meeting that had incarnated as a snake.

Nadoh

This world is full of evil doers. Save our family, 'O' Lord.

Sunyin

Mama, papa, you people gave me to a family of blood thirsty creatures that do not have the remotest respect for the value of human existence. Njenumeh even said I was lucky to have stayed alive in that area. He gave me certain herbs to chew to facilitate my exit from the compound. He also asked me to reveal all these secrets only to you. I have now completed my assignment. Never shall I set foot in the compound of Dohbani. I have returned safely to my parents, safe from evil spirits.

Njukebim

My ears are not convinced of what I have heard. I need proof. I need concrete evidence before I can be convinced. All of us shall go to Njenumeh tomorrow morning and let him reveal this again to us. At the moment I remain skeptical about what you people are saying.

Sunyin

I will go right now this mid-night and summon him here. (*Exits*)

Njukebim

Nadoh, I am sure you believe what your daughter has just told to you. My ignorance shall be completely wiped out if Njenumeh, the village seer in whom everyone trusts tells us himself. That all these things should be happening in this village and I, Njukebim, remain ignorant is unbelievable. If Njenumeh comes and reveals the whole incident to me as my daughter wants us to believe, then I will call myself a goat.

Nadoh

It is because of people like you that my daughter is going out at this time of the night to look for Njenumeh. Do you know what can happen to her on her way? So you strongly believe that your daughter has packed her things out of that compound only to come and deceive you? Is it because she is a woman? My husband, why are you the way you are? What can I really do to change you?

Njukebim

I did not send her out. I talked of tomorrow morning and since she was eager to go I couldn't stop her. You can keep on complaining. I will not stop until I know the truth. If Njenumeh comes here and confirms all what Sunyin has said, please carry me and dump me in a pit latrine, if you like. I still think she was exaggerating.

(*Enter Sunyin holding the hand of Njenumeh, followed closely by Toohtu the servant of Njenumeh*)

Njenumeh

Na wena compound this?

Sunyin

Yes papa (*Nadoh and Njukebim arrange a place for him to sit down*)

Njenumeh

You never tell dem say I no di shidon for chair?

Sunyin

Papa, he does not need a chair. He has his mat.

Njenumeh

Toohtu! Toohtu!

Toohtu

Oye

Njenumeh

Come gim me da …*bam shwi* quick. Na wena call me for yah?

Nadoh/Njukebim

(*In unison*)

Na we, papa.(*Njukebim makes a gesture to know what they should give as token for his visit*)

Njenumeh

Wena pekin nova tell wena say I no wan take anything for seka say thing dem dei plenti for tok? I no go take-am. Find kola chop becos wena pekin dong come back safe. (*A very absurd sound is heard from his bag. Gestures to Njukebim and Nadoh to come forward, examines their hands and nods. Throws down his cowries)* Na your husband this, Mami?

Nadoh
Yes papa.

Njenumeh
Your husband get trong heart so for sika weti noh? Yi no know say you be popo fine woman for yi? Yi no di hear weti weh you tell-am. Make yi try change from this bad fashion quick-quick.

Njukebim
Doh, me I no know say di fashion weh me I get am na bad one-o. Me I just dei like how man and yi woman fit dei. If na so, I go change as you talk.

Njenumeh
Try quick. Wena pekin come tell me just now say wena di call me for look again inside dat case for yi massa weyi dong die. Me I gree for come becos yesterday I see for ma pot other plenti ting weh I nobin tok for yi. Toohtu bring that mallam *(takes a mirror from him and examines it for a while)* I di see all ting now fine fine. Wena open ear fine.

Da popo pipo for 'Nda Saah' meeting na seven pipo. Two woman and five man pekin dem. Someone na da ya friend Loohfah weh you na yi di nak Nchibi drum, na dem di chop pipo. Da yi mimbo place wey dem di dance dey, na "Nda Saah". Loohfah di cut head for da pikin dem for dey. Na say you trong, like yi for dong take you. Someone na Ngangkwetbun weh you get farm weti yi for Njamke. Yi di shidong yi one for yi house. Na for sika say yi be dong give yi woman, pekin and papa for 'Nda Saah'. Yi dong get plenti money but da money na for kill other pipo.

Njukebim
Na so?

Njenumeh
Some one na da big Buhkap. Yi get plenti money wit big belle. Na yi two pekin dem wey don die so. All that yi business for road wey music di tok for dei so na "nda Saah". Yi woman sep no di born again. All yi friend dem dong run yi. Another one na da wena Nganglooti. Look da yi woman weh yi di sick so, dem dong call me for dei, I deny fo seka sey I know wehti dei dei.

Dem be tok for 'Nda Saah' meeting say make yi bring yi woman small time. Wena go hear say yi dong die; na yi massa go take- am. Then Loohfah weh yi get big motorcycle and four big motor for road. All da money comot from 'Nda Saah' weh when yi kill yi pepo dem dedi givam for yi. Nukemih na da snake wey yi kill Dohbani. Yi own work na for de waka look fine for find man pekin dem. Some di man pekin wey de di die so dey di tok all kind story, na Nukemih di kill am when yi sleep with dem. Yi own plenti money na for kill plenti pepo givam for 'Nda Saah'

Njukebim/Nadoh/Sunyin

(In unison)

Olu! Olulululu chei chei mawup!

Njenumeh

Wena dong forget Nahwubly? Da woman yi own plenti sotey yi fit flop bucket. All yi five pekin dem dong die. All dem dei for dei. Yi nobi fit come for burial for Dohbani becos yi no for fit see yi die body. Then yi come tok big lie for Sunyin. Yi dong chop all yi Mami and Papa dem and all pekin for yi Mami. Na yi wey, I bin tok say make wena pekin run quick from yi compound.

Sunyin

Papa yi bin give me some chain for my neck. I cut-am yesterday throway for bush.

Njenumeh

Da one nobin bad plenti becos na just for givam for any new marry woman.

Njukebim

I cannot believe my ears. I am now a changed husband. I cannot continue to stay with my family in such a morally rotten society. My family and I have to escape from this area.

Njenumeh

Man no run. Make we try do something for dem. Wuna agree make I kill dem all.

Njukebim/Nadoh/Sunyin

(In unison)

Kill dem!! Kill dem!!

Njenumeh

Toohtu fa miyi- *(gives him a long sword)*. I kill dem.

43

All

Kill dem papa for we and this village.

Njenumeh

I kill?

All

Kill!!!

Njenumeh

(Pierces the bag with the sword and hurriedly leaves the room with Toohtu)
(Exits)

Njukebim

So it is true. Never trust your neighbor or friend in this village. How could Loohfah, Ngangkwetbun, Buhkap, Nuhkemih, Nahwubly, Nganglooti, all of them, my closest associates, be blood thirsty villains? No wonder, Loohfah has tried all means to draw me into this meeting which he pretentiously calls 'Njangi'. My wife and daughter, do you people know that if not of my ceaseless prayer and commitment to God Almighty to protect my family, you could have found yourselves in the abstract world?

Nadoh/Sunyin

(In unison)

True.

Nadoh

So Loohfah and all the rest should find themselves comfortably in hell... *(The sound of the drum is heard. Njukebim makes a sign to her to shut up).*

(The sound of the drum grows louder. It is the village drum. All the seven members of 'Nda Saah' have died.)

(Enter Ngangtum the town crier)

Ngangtum

What are you still doing at home? The whole village has come out to see the bodies of seven strong individuals of the village who have suddenly died mysteriously. Go out to the palace and see for yourselves. *(They all rush out giving an ironical cry of sympathy)*

The End!